Twilight of the Jackass Prospector

Death Valley Area Portraits of the 1930's

Twilight of the Jackass Prospector
Death Valley Area Portraits of the 1930's

featuring photography by
Robert Ansel Cartter

introduction & text by
George R. Cartter

SAGEBRUSH PRESS • P.O. BOX 87 • MORONGO VALLEY, CA. 92256

COVER PHOTO: (left to right) Seldom Seen Slim, Walter Sorensen, Chris Wicht and Fred Grey in front of Fred Grey's home in Ballarat, 1935. All photographs in this work are by Robert A. Cartter, except as noted.

DEDICATION

This book is dedicated to Teresa and Emily Ann, that it might be a small window on part of their Old West desert heritage.

ACKNOWLEDGMENTS

Very special thanks to George Pipkin, Mojave Desert historian, for re-telling tales that helped the text along; to Tom Murray for his generosity with his photographs; to Myrtle Murchison for her helpful research; to Dan and Janet Cronkhite for their editorial assistance; to my wife, Marlene, for her general encouragement; and to Margaret Cartter, my father's wife, whose love and support got this project started again after his passing.

Introduction

Twenty light years out into the cosmos drifts the "Death Valley Days" television broadcasts hosted by Ronald Reagan. The Old West is long gone. The realities have dissolved into memories, histories, and legends. The whole image of Death Valley has changed from a hot and hard stop over for gold seekers and Shoshone Indians to a stark, but artistic Hollywood backdrop.

The gold and silver strikes above Post Office Springs played out in the late nineteen teens, and the back door was closed on the Great California Gold Rush. The Death Valley area's population had peaked between 1905 and 1908, when thousands worked the rocks around Skidoo and Rhyolite. By the 1930's that population had boiled down to those relative few who were at home on the sage range or in the canyons above the salt flats. Most of the working burros had been given their unconditional release. New conveyances and contrivances had greatly mitigated desert problems like rattlesnake bites, rock slides, flash floods, and The Heat. By the late 1920's folks had taken to venturing motor tours of the Valley.

In 1936 Charlie Chaplin presented "Modern Times" for the big screen. It was "Modern Times", but it was also a silent movie, one foot still in a nearly bygone era. So it was at the same time with the Mojave old-timers. Younger people made their livings differently. More people worked for somebody else. And whatever they did, they usually drove an automobile to the place where they did it. They moved faster. The Old West had all but flickered out, the last of its characters were in retirement, yet still a living part of those days of jackass prospectors, oxen-drawn wagons, and Shoshone sovereignty.

Most of the photographs in this book were taken between 1930 and 1940 by my father. Some have appeared in other publications, while others are published here for the first time. The pictures were not taken as part of a preconceived project. Indeed, it is fifty years or so after the shutter closed on these scenes that they are being bound together. Two important photographs included here are courtesy of Tom G. Murray. His fine shot of Death Valley Scotty has never before been published.

The accompanying descriptions were written from comments and stories of my father's, with help from the sources listed in the bibliography and conversations with Death Valley and Searles Valley old-timer and author George Pipkin, co-owner and manager of Wildrose Station in the 1940's. The blame is mine for any historical inaccuracies that I may have passed along.

What is meant to be presented here are some of the last images of the Old West, images carried aways into the twentieth century by a few old Shoshone Indians and a few old jackass prospectors. I hope the reader enjoys these character representations of a fascinating era as it faded away.

George R. Cartter
AZUSA, CALIFORNIA
SUMMER, 1982

Twilight of the Jackass Prospector

Death Valley Area Portraits of the 1930's

Indian George (Bah-vanda-sava-nu-kee—*Boy Who Runs Away*)

The men looked strange and their accouterments were strikingly non-Indian. The oxen with them were animals the young Shoshone boy had never seen. Later to be known as Indian George, the nine-year-old watched the small party of men work their way up a waterless canyon, struggling in their pursuit of a passage out of Death Valley and over the Panamint Mountains. The Shoshone boy related the sight to his elders. They told him that word of these kind of people had come from a neighboring Shoshone group to the northeast. Some of them had killed two Shoshonis by the unfamiliar process of gunfire. The strangers would be avoided.

Members of the Manly-Bennett party, or the Jayhawkers, or any of the splinter groups of the Sand Walking Company that discovered Death Valley on their 1849 Gold Rush itinerary, would have found information on mountain passes and water sources very valuable. When the earlier strangers shot down the hope of local hospitality, the stage was set for young Indian George to witness the grievous desert drama of 1849 as it continued to unfold.

The Indian Ranch at Warm Springs

In 1781 the Yuma Indians repulsed an attempted Spanish invasion of their homeland. The Spanish had hoped to set up some inland missions along the Colorado River. With the defeat at Yuma, they abandoned the project as too costly. Spanish and Mexican interests in coastal California never carried them to Death Valley. Sixty-five years or so after the Yuma-Spanish battles, John C. Fremont was exploring eastern California, but The Pathfinder skirted Tomesha, "Ground Afire", later to be known as Death Valley. In late 1849 the small, isolated community of people in the very southwest corner of the greater Shoshone nation still had never seen any non-Indians. Then came the story of the Boy Who Runs Away, named for his reaction to those strangers of '49.

Some aspects of the old economy survived into the twentieth century. Pinon nuts, mesquite beans, chuckawalla stew, and bighorn sheep steaks were still part of the fare. Raising Angora goats, gold and silver prospecting and guiding greenhorns through the country came along as new occupations.

An "Indian Ranch" remains, but the community of Panamint Indians is gone now.

Shoshone Johnny

One of the great mines in Rhyolite, Nevada, was called the Montgomery-Shoshone mine. It wasn't far from the famous Bullfrog mine, where in 1905 these two mines paced the gold boom in the district.

The story goes that Bob Montgomery paid Shoshone Johnny two dollars and a brand new pair of bib overalls for the claim Johnny had staked. Five million dollars in gold came out of that Montgomery-Shoshone mine in the next few years.

In later years Shoshone Johnny wintered at Furnace Creek, occasionally posing for photographers at fifty cents a shot. As the Panamint Shoshonis had generally done for a long, long time, he spent his summers up in the cooler clime of Wildrose Canyon.

Jim Boyles

Jim Boyles (at left in the picture) was the unofficial agent of the Panamint Indians, helping to handle some of their dealings with the Bureau of Indian Affairs. He was also Trona's butcher. After serving in World War I, he worked as a pipeline rider, doing horseback patrol of the water line from the Argus Range to Trona, plugging the little holes the alkali might eat in the pipes and keeping that precious desert water flowing.

Billy Hyder

This man was a hat salesman. He had worked in a small haberdashery in Los Angeles. Then came his divorce settlement. He felt that the terms of it stemmed from a most improper relationship between his former wife and the presiding judge. He couldn't stand it.

Billy Hyder arrived at the foot of the Panamint Mountains in a tuxedo, changed his clothes and then spent twenty years prospecting in the Death Valley region. He saw flivvers rise and burros fade, but he found no gold. He struck neither silver nor lead, searching twenty years in vain for any kind of vein. He died a poor, but well liked prospector. Billy did, however, leave behind a small fortune in alimony obligations.

Frank "Shorty" Harris (with Indian George)

Shorty was known for the telling of prospecting tales. He was with Ed Cross when they found a green rock outcropping laced with gold that became the famous Bullfrog mine near Rhyolite. He was headed to Ballarat for a Fourth of July celebration in 1905 with Pete Aguereberry when Pete showed him some rich ore that eventually put the mining camp of Harrisburg on the map. There were other finds and people listened to his stories. A partner might throw a fit as he spread word of a precious new find, but the stories might also drive up the price for rights to a claim. Shorty sold claims, he worked them as little as necessary. He also changed partners often.

His epitaph is Death Valley famous: "Here lies Shorty Harris, a single blanket jackass prospector, 1856-1934."

—Tom G. Murray Collection

Seldom Seen Slim (Charles Ferge)

Seldom Seen Slim did not hesitate to bill himself as the last of the jackass prospectors. He had roamed the Valley of Death and the surrounding mountains prospecting with the likes of Shorty Harris and Jim Sherlock. His self-appointed title and the nostalgia it relates to brought a national network television crew to Ballarat for his funeral in 1968.

Grizzled old jackass prospectors conjure up visions of sparkling ore samples being chipped from a remote rock ledge, or gunfights with prospective claim jumpers. Most of the people who knew Slim could more easily command visions of soap and water. Slim would have very little to do with either. The writer's Aunt Alice worked at a Trona store where Slim would come for supplies, once a month or so. He might boast that he'd bathed twice in the preceding year, but Aunt Alice sensed no such frequent washing. Seldom Seen Slim was a champion to kids who didn't like to take baths, a legend in his own grime. Slim was the sole resident of Ballarat for many years, having maintained a ripe age for a long time.

Jim Sherlock

At the turn of the century there was a mining promoter who held a well respected speed record for a run from Ballarat to Los Angeles by horse team and wagon. Jim Sherlock challenged that record in 1903 with his wagon and his team of burros. Because of Jim's reputation as an ex-gunslinger and gambler out of the Wyoming territory, the guffaws and jackass jokes were doubtlessly kept to a minimum, but Jim did have to cover a lot of heavy bets against his setting any new record by pushing donkeys all the way to L.A.

Bets down, Jim and his team hit the road. When the course went around a mountain range, Jim unbolted his wagon, folded it up, and packed the whole thing on his burros. They went straight over the mountains. The accordian wagon maneuver put Jim Sherlock, his team and wagon into the City of Angels a whole day ahead of the fastest horse and wagon time.

Panamint City

Panamint City, up in Surprise Canyon, high on the rim of Death Valley, was a boom town whose life was hard, fast, and wild. In 1873, the district's mines were going to rival the Comstock Lode in silver production. In 1876 a flash flood destroyed fifteen Panaminters and much of the young town, already past its prime.

Packed into Panamint's brief tour in the silver spotlight were lots of high grade, yet hard rock strikes. Two United States Senators were sinking lots of money into mine speculation. A bandit firm, Small and MacDonald, made regular professional visits, occasionally dabbling in Robin Hoodism. Hundreds of Chinese workers and a few opium dens resided just down the canyon from a very experienced Maiden Lane. Sour Dough Gulch held most of the fifty-some local victims of "lead poisoning", runners-up to a verdict of "self defense."

Abandoned for thirty years, but still intact, the pool table in Dave Neagle's Oriental Saloon was one part of old Panamint that rolled on into the twentieth century. Gold strikes above Post Office Springs excited Ballarat in 1905 and gave Chris Wicht the cue to haul the aged, but serviceable billiard green down Surprise Canyon and install it as a popular feature in his own saloon.

Cloudburst on the Mojave (looking toward Inyokern)

Surprise Canyon
Aug. 7, '41

Dear Bob,

Both your letters to hand and about time I answered as I don't know when I will get another chance to send out any mail as we have just been visited by a cloudburst and a big one. washed the road out completely to mouth of canyon. The Thompsons walked in this morning so will send this out by them. . . . will take me at least a month to fix road unless get some help. out side of this bad luck I am feeling fine and hope you are getting along fine.

With our kindest,
Chris and Bonnie

P.S. We sure miss you

Death Valley area folks have a standard line on the region's summer climate: "A hunerd an' twenty in the shade and there ain't no shade." The rain, in its own way, can visit in as harsh a style as the summer sun. Cloudburst water falls in sheets, erosion goes to work at a frantic pace and a flash flood can develop quickly in a canyon or ravine.

The above letter is from Chris Wicht to Robert Cartter. Chris took personal responsibility for the road to Panamint City.

Chris Wicht

In the back of his saloon, in the back of his pants, Chris Wicht took a bullet from his own gun late one night in 1903. Chris had fancied the friendship of a Randsburg woman who was also another man's flame. She had once rebuffed Chris' fancying by stabbing him in the chest with a pair of scissors. The wound was on the mend when a late hour found the trio and their passions alone at the bar. Chris ordered the Other Man out of his saloon at gunpoint. A scuffle ensued, the Other Man got the pistol and then got Chris as he attempted a back door retreat.

Hearing the ruckus, Fred Grey came running from his assay office across the street to find Chris clutching his broken heart (the scissor wound had opened up a bit). Fred easily saved Chris. The saloon survived until about 1917 and Chris lived on in Surprise Canyon until 1944, but that desert love triangle came to a painful end that night back in '03.

⌒ Fred Grey

Fred would do a little prospecting, but he kept it to a minimum. Fred had a college education in geology and ran an assaying business in Ballarat, serving those thinned out ranks of prospectors and miners still working the Panamints and Death Valley area. He lived in or around the town for 45 years.

Fred was known to have first aided Chris Wicht through a bleeding, broken heart affair. He made critical repairs, at his own expense, of the small Warm Springs aqueduct that served to give the Indian Ranch a rustic oasis status. In the days when gold strikes east of town lent a little life to the place, Fred Grey was respected as the honorary mayor of Ballarat.

Death Valley Scotty (Walter Scott)

As Indian George was a link between a last corner of the old Shoshone nation and modern times, Walter Scott was one who tied a lot of the new, glittering Hollywood hyperbole to the image of the Death Valley jackass prospector. Of course, Scotty wasn't really a jackass prospector on two counts. The first was that Scotty was quite partial to mules, not burros, for packing and riding. The second count was the main count, which was the bank account of Chicago financier Albert Johnson. Scotty's castle stands as a monument to Mr. Johnson's greenback deposits and Walter Scott's performance as a chief Death Valley character, a former star of Buffalo Bill's Wild West Show who had struck a claim to desert royalty.

Scotty's Castle

The wrought iron weather vanes on the towers at Scotty's Castle are meant to be silhouettes of Scotty and a burro out prospecting. Walter Scott worked his Knickerbocker claim near Hidden Springs for a wealth of publicity and a hot mystique. Some say the location possessed less gold than your uncle Henry's teeth. Scotty felt it was so rich that its exact location had to be kept secret.

When this picture was taken in the mid 1930's, Scotty lived at the Death Valley Ranch and his partner, Albert Johnson, visited regularly. The swimming pool wasn't finished yet and the palm trees imported from San Bernardino were dead but still standing. A person could tour the place for a dollar.

Mengel's Butte Valley Home

Carl Mengel's place at Greater View Spring in Butte Valley provided an outstanding view of the Funeral Mountains to the east and easy access to his gold diggings in Goler Wash.

Carl had two claims in Goler Wash, one he bought in 1912 and a better one he discovered while trying to figure out a trail to help develop the first claim. He had settled in Butte Valley while recovering from a mining accident and worked those claims until not long before his death in 1944.

Carl Mengel

Carl Mengel was born in San Bernardino, California in 1868 to German immigrant parents. He spent well over half his life prospecting and mining in the eastern Mojave.

One day he and another man were analyzing some ore in a mine when a large section of the tunnel gave way, trapping Carl. A huge piece of rock crushed his leg. By the time rescuers reached Carl, two doctors had been summoned to the scene and they were able to save his life.

One account (the photographer's) was that Carl was uncertain of the fate of his companion or the status of any rescue attempt. There was no way for Carl to move the boulder that was pinning him to the floor of the mine. It was a grim, classic case of being stuck between a rock and a hard place. After checking his options, he tied a tourniquet around his ankle and with his knife, he amputated that portion of his foot that was crushed under the boulder. Eventually, he was free of that mine.

Whatever the exact circumstances of the mine accident, Carl was known by many as Peg Leg Mengel.

Pete Aguereberry

Only a few prospectors had a gold or silver mine. Most would try to find some high grade ore (or borrow some) and then sell the rights to the claim. Other people were supposed to do the hard rock, hard work mining, and gamble that the ore hadn't come from an isolated pocket.

Pete, with Shorty Harris, made the Harrisberry strike. He kept a good claim in the area, fighting off claim jumpers and shyster lawyers. When he felt a pay day was due, he would go in and knock some ore out of that Eureka mine. He did that for nearly forty years, taking odd jobs, now and then, for their social rewards.

Aguereberry Point is named after Pete. He valued the view of Death Valley from there and had wanted it to be his final resting place. Ironically, the 1933 Monument status of Death Valley disallowed Aguereberry Point as Pete's monument and he was interred at Mount Whitney Cemetery in Lone Pine.

Ambroise Aguereberry

Ambroise Aguereberry was the nephew of Pete Aguereberry. In the 1930's Ambroise left his job as a waiter in Los Angeles to help his uncle Pete work the Eureka mine. Ambroise had fought in World War I with the French army and served with the American army in World War II. He returned to work the Eureka after the war. Pete had passed away in 1945, so Ambroise worked alone. The solitude, including a six-week long period of isolation resulting from a Panamint snow storm in 1948, was hard on Ambroise, and he eventually had to leave the region. He made a trip back to his native France, visited his Basque homeland, then returned for good to Southern California. Ambroise Aguereberry's final resting place is the Los Angeles National Cemetery in Sawtelle.

Harry Hughes

Harry Hughes didn't want anybody to write about him, maintaining that he was of British royalty and would be returned to England if his whereabouts were known. He wanted to stay in the Mojave, a loner.

There was also the matter of his having shot a man to death in Bruce Canyon in an argument over a burro. No witnesses. "Self defense" declared the judge. George Pipkin says that he couldn't detect any of old Harry's British accent when he knew him in the 1930's.

Walter Sorensen

Walter Sorensen was jovial, well liked locally, a dealer in mining claims, often in and out of the area. He drove away from Panamint Valley one day to make his home in Lone Pine. Rich, romantic tales about Walter don't abound at all.

Twenty Mule Team Borax Run (A 1937 Re-enactment)

Someone might count the mules in the picture and start worrying about their laundry not getting as bright and clean as advertised because there's only sixteen mules there. Well, that's the way it was in the 1880's. If the run could be made with sixteen or a dozen mules, that's all that were hitched up. Behind the two borax wagons with their over-sized wheels, a third tank wagon carried a supply of water for those working mules. The optimum number of animals varied with the load, the route, and the weather, and it wasn't wise or profitable to deviate much from the appropriate size team.

The Teamster handled the mules using a "jerk line" that was attached to their harnesses. His helper, The Swamper, managed the brake, fed and watered the team, and was the general trouble shooter. Teamsters and swampers shouted lots of commands and curses. If one mule can be stubborn, twenty or even a dozen could be a mighty strong source of frustration. The desert silence was broken often and the "Mule Skinner Blues" is a song that was first sung a long time ago.

Ed Teagle

In the 1890's, when the Teagle brothers, Ed and Charley, took over the Garden Station freight business, established by old John Searles, the tall freight wagons were pulled by mule teams. By the mid 1920's the Searles Lake to Randsburg run was a two hour truck drive. Built as a stop over on the two day trip of mule team wagons, Teagle's midway station had become romantic, but obsolete Old West stuff.

With years of experience hauling mining supplies and ore through the eastern Mojave, how did this respectable freighter resist the turn-of-the-century gold fever epidemic in the hills? He didn't. Ed Teagle, pictured here in the 1930's in the colonnade of Trona's Austin Hall, had the Stockwell Mine in the Slate Range.

Slate Range Crossing

Coming up over the pass between the Slate Range and the Argus Mountains from the southwest, one looks across Panamint Valley towards the Panamint Mountains, the western barrier of Death Valley. Forty-niners perished in these Slate mountains, little less harsh for the desert foot traveler than Death Valley itself. Many of the region's miners and prospectors came to Trona for supplies and returned over this Slate Range Crossing to reseek their fortunes. The road was originally built by Chinese labor and provided a short cut to Los Angeles from the rich Panamint City mines.

Ben Harrison & his Roaming Cowboys

On August 12, 1939, while Indian George, Carl Mengel, and Pete Aguereberry were playing out their days in the Panamints and around Death Valley, Ben Harrison and his Roaming Cowboys played electronically amplified country music from a float anchored in the huge salt water pool at Valley Wells. The occasion was the company picnic and water carnival for Trona's potash and chemical workers, an annual, post-prohibition summer beer bust.

The band played "Away Out There" and tunes about horses, loves lost, open spaces and "Listen to the Mockingbird." Their cowboy music themes still related then to the old-timers living a few miles north beyond the Slate Range.

Robert Ansel Cartter (on Telescope Peak)

Robert Cartter came to Searles Valley in 1930. He hadn't lived in the desert since the family raised turkeys in Mojave in the early nineteen teens. Most of his youth was spent on orange ranches in southern and central California. Working at a small assay office in Los Angeles in 1930, not enough ore was coming in to pay his wages, so Bob hired on at the potash plant in Trona.

Robert spent much of his free time at Chris Wicht's place on the road to Panamint City. He helped Chris build a cement pond for watering his burros. He got to know a number of the Death Valley old-timers and sometimes took his camera along on visits. His photographs have appeared in a variety of publications.

Bob left the desert in 1951 with a wife and child, after spending World War II in the Yukon and on the Aleutian Islands. He went to work at the Lever Brothers plant in suburban Los Angeles. His photography became confined to family snapshots, while he developed into a prize winning gem cutter and jeweler.

THE AUTHOR
Trona, California
1949

Bibliography

Death Valley Men by Bourke Lee. The MacMillan Co., N.Y., 1932.

Silver Stampede by Neill C. Wilson. The MacMillan Co., N.Y., 1937.

Death Valley Guide by Federal Writers Project, Works Progress Administration of Northern California. Houghton Mifflin Co., Boston, 1939.

Death Valley and Its Country by George Palmer Putnam. Duell, Sloan & Pearce, N.Y., 1946.

Loafing Along Death Valley Trails by William Caruthers. Death Valley Publishing Co., Ontario, Calif. 1951.

Desert Bonanza by Marcia Rittenhouse Wynn. The Arthur H. Clark Co., Glendale, Calif., 1963.

Ballarat by Hubbard, Bray and Pipkin. Published by Paul and Arline Hubbard, Lancaster, Calif., 1965.

Seldom Seen Slim by Tom G. Murray. Published by the author, San Fernando, Calif., 1971.

Death Valley's Victims by Daniel Cronkhite. Sagebrush Press, Morongo Valley, Calif., 1980.

Place Names of the Death Valley Region in California and Nevada by T. S. Palmer. Sagebrush Press, Morongo Valley, Calif., 1980.

Pete Aguereberry by George C. Pipkin. Murchison Publications, Trona, Calif., 1982.

Index

This first printing of *Twilight of the Jackass Prospector* has been limited to 2,000 copies. The text type is 12 point Linotype Granjon with special refinement and olde style characters; display type is Monotype Deepdene. Typography and design is by the Sagebrush Press, Morongo Valley, Calif.